The Devil's Dictionary Of Wall Street

Michael Silverstein

Table Of Contents

Michael Silverstein

Introduction

THE DEVIL'S DICTIONARY is a classic of misanthropic American literature. It was written in bits and pieces between 1881 and 1906 by Ambrose Bierce, a well-known social critic, short story writer, editor, columnist, gossip, arbiter of West Coast taste and fashion, and all-purpose cynic.

At a time when most Americans were exhibiting an almost pathological positivism, Bierce, and his great contemporary Mark Twain, were taking an opposite tack. The result was some of the most truthful and incisive (which is to say derisive and satirical) word-smithing ever spawned by a New World culture.

Between 1909 and 1912 some million words of Bierce's enormous writing output was organized into twelve volumes of collected works. Volume VII of this collection was published in 1911 under the title THE DEVIL'S DICTIONARY. Parts of this book have been consciously and unconsciously plagiarized by social commentators ever since.

THE DEVIL'S DICTIONARY is actually a grab-bag of delights and trivia. Mixed with its brilliant satire and sophisticated malice are outright silliness, period bigotry, and a lot of the sort of filler that creeps in whenever a good editor is not on hand to winnow. Along with acerbic definitions it features poems, dialogues, and asides by Bierce's exorbitantly contrived alter ego, Father Gassalasca Jape, S.J.

The best Bierce definitions involve politics, religion and the law. In the former category he characterizes patriots as "the dupes of statesmen and the tools of conquerors," and peace as "a period of cheating between two periods of fighting." On religion, he defines a Christian as "one who follows the teachings of Christ in so far as they are not inconsistent with a life of sin," and calls a saint "a dead sinner, revised and edited." His description of litigation is "a machine in which you go into as a pig and come out as a sausage." Clearly, the mind at work here is one that still merits a place on contemporary bookshelves.

One important part of the human comedy in which Bierce was largely silent, however, was the realm of finances. Of the 1,000-odd definitions found in the 1911 DEVIL'S DICTIONARY, only a dozen or so relate directly to this subject. Of this small number only a very few are clever and timeless enough to appeal to present-day readers.

In this limited category, Wall Street is summed up as "a symbol of sin for every devil to rebuke," and Mammon is claimed to be "the God of the world's leading religion...(with)...his chief temple in the holy city of New York."

Had this deep-seeing man lived in our time, he doubtless would have favored us with many more definitions in this realm. Alas, Ambrose Gwinett Bierce, like King Arthur and Judge Crater, is no longer around to do the job. This singular individual expired (or at least passed from public view) in a way that was much in keeping with his most unusual life. Sometime in 1913 a still chipper 71-year-old Bierce heard that a revolution was brewing in Mexico and decided to travel there for a first-hand look at the action. One morning he rode off with some rebel horsemen and was never heard from again.

In his absence it seems only right to offer some Bierce-like devilish definitions of players and games in our own high finance ravaged era. And with this in mind.....

Some Financial
Definitions For Our Times

A

Abenomics:
Japan's souped up version of The Fed's quantitative easing policy, which many people think will lead to an Abegeddon. (See also Bernankenomics and Bonkernomics)

Analysts:
Referees of asset values who are often, indeed usually, employed by institutions with a stake in having asset values deemed more valuable.

Annual Reports:
Weighty documents churned out in large numbers whose purpose in this Internet Age seems little more than a subsidy to a bankrupt postal system.

Appreciation:
The increase in the value of an asset; and/or, what you feel when an analyst (See above) says an asset that you own has increased in value.

Asia's Tigers:
Eastern hemisphere powerhouses that have outgrown their
Walmart nurturing stage of economic life.

Austerity:
A very unpleasant economic state of affairs brought about by
people claiming they are trying to prevent a very unpleasant
economic state of affairs.

Autarky:
A national economic policy built around the song, "I Did It My
Way;" a national policy currently only practiced diligently by
North Korea.

Ayn Rand:
A writer whose economic theories actually somehow managed to
be more poorly constructed than her fiction.

B
_____

Baby Boomers:
The last generation to enjoy an American economic boom that
lasted more than half-a-century, a group closely followed by the
American baby busters generation.

Balance Sheets:
Debit on the left, credit on the right, make 'em, somehow, come
out right.

Bank Bailouts:
Attempting to clean the Augean stables of finance without
removing the stable defilers.

Bank Regulators:
Goldman Sachs employees on sabbatical leave.

Bank Reserves:
Large sums of money that grow ever larger as The Fed pumps out more in the vain hope that some will actually be loaned to deserving enterprises.

Bankruptcy:
A legal mechanism   that once allowed   individuals to start over, but which has now been "reformed" into a legal mechanism that ensures these same individuals remain in peonage to their lenders.

Bargain Hunters:
Investors who believe that in spite of evidence to the contrary, any security priced near zero must have a residual or unrealized value and is therefore worth acquiring. (See also Faith-Based Investing and Dead Dog Bounce.)

Bear Market:
A stock market not artificially inflated by quantitative easing.

Ben (Bernanke), Larry (Summers) And Tim (Geithner):
Present day incarnations of Moe, Larry and Curley .

Ben Bernanke:
A water carrier for the British army in India was the hero of Kipling's poem, 'Gunga Din.' For years Fed Chairman Ben Bernanke has been carrying the water for Wall Streeters. Here, then, is a poem celebrating the Fed Chairman's service to his prime constituency.

Bernankenomics:
An economic theory that holds that if you print enough money, something good is bound to happen. (SEE also Abenomics)

Best And Brightest:
Dumb and dumber on Wall Street in thousand dollar suits.

———————

Gunga Ben

You may praise free market's power
With stocks in endless flower
And home prices looking like they'll never top;
But comes the sound of crashing
There's just one place you're a'looking
And a'begging for the horrid drop to stop.

Sure you spend your working time
In that well-paid Wall Street clime
Claimin' you're a master of the universe;
And the crew you bring together
Swears you need no outside fetter
'Til your arrogance brings down that crashing curse.

Then it's "Ben! Ben! Ben!
We need a huge Fed handout once again;"
Though all others he's ignorin'
For you guys Ben is adorin'
Always saving The Street's bacon, Gunga Ben.

———————

Beta:
A measure of stock volatility, as in the phrase, "mine is beta than yorz."

Bitcoins:
Computer-generated money with no discernible backing except
the faith of those who view it as valuable — rather like the huge
new pile of fiat money being created by panicked central bankers,
except that there's a limit on the amount of Bitcoins that will be
issued and no such limit on what's churned out by central bank
printing presses

Blame Game: (SEE: Default)

Bond Rating Agencies:
Credit deal enablers whose clients are expected to show
appropriate monetary gratitude.

Bonkernomics:
The only name that really describes the Rube Goldberg-like
economic concoctions being served up to suffering populations by
central bankers who have run out of other ideas.

Bonuses: (SEE: Wall Street Bonuses)

Bottom Line:
Corporate behavior so bad it can't go any lower.

BRICs:
Brazil, Russia, India and China; the four largest economies
in what is often referred to as "the emerging world" by
commentators in countries such as our own whose own economies
are no longer emerging but sinking fast.

Broker: Having less than you had before by virtue of listening to
someone whose own "broker" job title should have let you know
in advance that this was what you could expect.

Bull Market:
Append the usual ending to "bull" and you'll have a good feel for
what this market is build on.

C

Capital Gains:
In the ongoing competition with labor, this is a status report

Central Bankers:
The people ultimately in charge of solving the problems they
ultimately created. Do they inspire you with confidence that they
will succeed, or do they actually come across as...

Central Banks:
Financial institutions that are part of governments whose primary
function these days is supporting privately owned investment
banks in every way possible.

Frightened
Little Men

They meet to shape our daily lives,
Our economic masters;
To even out the nasty blips,
And shield us from disasters.

The media are reverent
'Bout what these men all teach;
Assuring us, they know the way,
Toward ends we yearn to reach.

But as I watch more carefully,
I see what I've long feared;
These masters of economies
Seem little men—and scared.

CEOs:
Individuals who somehow contrive to not only receive
huge compensation for successful work, but also get huge
compensation when they fail and are forced to resign. All things
considered, I guess we'd all like to be...

Christmas:
Formerly a religious holiday that has morphed into a seasonal
obligation to overspend.

Churning (a.k.a. High Frequency Trading):
Stock trading by Wall Street banks and other institutions that have
no purpose but generating fees for traders, or tapping into very
short-term movements in stock prices that have no relation to the
underlying health of the companies whose stock is being traded.

Collateral:
Something of real value a borrower has to put to get a loan, except
if the borrower is a Wall Street bank and the loan comes from The
Fed in which case real value is no longer required.

College Debt:
The financial hangover from a four-year campus smoker that no
amount of Alka-Seltzer and aspirin can make go away.

Commissions (a.k.a. Commish):
Rewards for helping sell products your employer wants you to
sell, products you often know in your heart you would personally
never buy.

Corporate Boards:
Men who play golf with CEOs, and receive large sinecures for
attending occasional meetings where large increases in these
CEOs' compensation packages are approved.

Home On The
CEO's Range

Oh, give me a home,
Where the CEOs roam,
And the sky is the limit on pay;
Where you never get fired,
By a board that you hired,
And they're glad pers'nal costs to defray.

Please, get it arranged,
Get me placed where a boss ain't short-changed;
I'll be an achiever,
Such a job-cutting beaver,
Employees will think I'm deranged.

Oh, give me a home,
Where the CEOs roam,
And big tax hits don't make a guy weep;
Where if you can hack it,
A sweet option packet,
Will let you avoid bracket creep.

Please, get it arranged,
Get me placed where a boss ain't short-changed;
I'll work like a beaver,
A reiver with fever,
From profits you'll ne'er be estranged.

Counterparty:
The guy you're trying to outsmart in a financial deal.

Counterfeiting:
An illegal practice involving the creation of false wealth by private individuals; this may be contrasted (or not contrasted) to the perfectly legal practice of false wealth creation that occurs when the Federal Reserve prints excessive amounts of money. (SEE: Quantitative Easing)

Counter-Intuitive Thinking:
Currently a popular Wall Street nostrum for addressing problems of various kinds; such thinking holds that what is sensible and obvious is less true than what is clearly idiotic; one example of this thinking involves emissions trading that allows polluters to buy the right to pollute in the belief that this will reduce pollution.

COW (Concentration of Wealth):
The ultimate cause of all problems in first world economies, but a cause that is never addressed for fear of offending large contributors to the campaigns of politicians who run first world economies.

Creative Destruction:
The destruction of a competitor's business that comes about because it no longer meets a real market need — to be clearly differentiated from destruction of your own enterprise, which only occurs due to bad luck, market downturns, or acts of God.

Credit Default Swaps:
Insurance on loans that probably shouldn't have been made in the first place, with this insurance backed by insurers who might not be able to pay up if these loans go sour.

Credit Score:
What Americans receive these days in return for giving up their right to privacy.

Cyprus:
A small country whose partners in the EU didn't think its
economy was too-big-to-fail — so they failed it.

D

Dead Cat Bounce (Also rendered Dead Dog Bounce by people
who can't bear the thought of a cat dying):
A Wall Street term that describes when bargain hunters (See
definition above) spot an apparently worthless security and buy it
up, thus causing its price to rise. (Also see Faith-based Investing)

Death Tax: (SEE: Estate Tax)

Debt Ceiling:
The missing roof atop a national house of cards that keeps people
inside dry until it rains.

Debtor Nation:
A country that can not control its appetites or live within its
means and must therefore resort to exorbitant taxation or currency
debasement to stay afloat; nations in this category today include
Chad, Haiti, Belize, Kampuchea, Ukraine and the United States of
America, not necessarily in that order of irresponsibility.

Debt Relief:
The pause that refreshes

Default:
Sometin' de udder guy dun.

Delinquency:
A modest bit of bad behavior by young people caught smoking

marijuana, or by their parents when missing a credit card payment.

Depletion Allowance:
A gift given to mining and petroleum firms for despoiling the environment.

Depreciation:
A theoretical lessening of an asset's value over time, even when the value of this asset in the real world is increasing.

Depression:
With apologies to William Yeats...

Derivative:
A kind of insurance issued by market mavens who have passed on the risk, the responsibility for paying up in case of a problem, to someone who may or may not be able do so — if indeed is even located.

Detroit's Big Three:
Poverty, property abandonment, insolvency.

Dividends:
Money you get for doing nothing but having money.

Double Dip:
A two-stage market decline with an upside in the middle during which suckers are encouraged to put in savings they will lose in the second dip.

Double Irish:
A technique used by some American companies to lessen their taxes by funneling profits through one Ireland-based subsidiary which then funnels it to another Irish subsidiary in ways that take advantage of convoluted Irish tax laws. A popular variant of this finagle is the Dutch Irish Dutch sandwich. All such techniques,

while legal, are inherently scummy and deserving of total contempt.

Downsizing:
A process that attempts to shoehorn a size 12 company work load into a size 10 workforce.

Due Diligence:
The prudent analysis of a deal's worth — a process no longer necessary when you do a swap (See definition below) that transfers the risk to another party. Due diligence takes time, skill and knowledge, while swapping involves just finding someone who believes you've actually done due diligence and wants a swap fee for accepting a deal's risk.

The Dreaded
Double Dip

There are few worse fears among the seers who give guidance to The Street,
Than an upward turn they claimed to discern that suddenly beats a retreat.
Then to save their reps, with practiced steps, they quickly do a back flip,
And loudly amend: "This might portend, the dreaded double dip."
Just as camels can have a single hump or be burdened down with two,
Economies sometimes follow a path that resembles a double-u;
And just when you think the worst is behind and profits are set to soar,
The edifice takes another lurch and you're worse off than before.
I've not come by to ruin your day with news of a sad Second Coming;
Indeed, such seer-like word display strikes me as unbecoming.
I'll only state, that the usual fate, that follows a glimmer-based bubble,
Is a market that trips, and double dips, to clear out its leftover rubble.

_____

The Next
Depression

Sinking and sinking in a sickening swirl,
Retail sales fall short of retailer goals;
Stock prices slide, well-run businesses fold;
Massive layoffs raise unemployment fears;
A loose-lipped faith in endless growth has died,
Replaced by loud cries for costly bailouts;
Good deals lack all support, while ponzi schemes
Quickly acquire devoted followings.

Surely, the Invisible Fist is clenched;
Surely, the Next Depression has begun.
The Next Depression! Just the sound of these words
With their intimations of Social Upheavals
Scares me witless! all my senses tell me that
Some long neglected institution,
A festering fiscal running sore,
Is inching toward the edge, the black hole point
Where lies unreel to reveal hidden deserts.
Economic cycles rule: but all know
That after long years of smug indulgence
Our expectations have become too fiercely fixed
And though still cosseted in hope filled dreams,
Wake'ning soon, a beastly age will dawn.

_____

E

Economic Boom:
A lot of economic activity, almost always excessive and short-lived, preceded and followed by the inevitable economic busts.

Economic Competitiveness:
I can work cheaper than you.

Economic Contraction: (SEE: Economic Growth)

Economic Forecasting:
Hindsight projected into the future.

Economic Growth:
In recent years, a characteristic of an economy in which the rich get richer and the standard of living of everyone else stays the same; this may be contrasted with an economic contraction, during which the rich get still richer but the standard of living of everyone else gets worse.

Economic Reality:
The morning after when everyone promises that "next time we won't believe that this time it's different."

Economic Recovery:
A period when things get worse more slowly between two periods when they get worse very quickly.

Economists:
People with a unique ability to be believed always in spite of almost never being right more than half the time. What causes this inability to do better?

Emissions Trading: (SEE: Counter-Intuitive Thinking)

The Problem
With Economists

An economist is a brilliant chap
Who studies the markets hard and long,
Which raises this question in many minds:
Why is he much of the time so wrong?

After giving this matter considerable thought
And pondering why the condition persists,
I conclude it comes down to a single fault:
He listens to other economists.

Entitlements:
Depending on your politics, either what you paid for and deserve,
or what you finagled from your economic betters at the ballot box.

Estate Tax:
A form of government predation that obliges trustafarians to earn
an honest living sooner than they would have done otherwise after
blowing through their inheritances.

Euro:
Some good ideas just don't work out well. Like the Edsel. Or the
single currency of the European Union.

European Union (a.k.a. EU):
A group of nations temporarily strung together by the curious
notion that a shared economic future of members with vastly
different economic, cultural and social norms is desirable, much
less possible.

Executive Bonuses: The modern economy-based equivalent
of the medieval droit du seigneur — that the guy at the top (it's
almost always a guy) gets first crack at things that rightfully
belong to others — you know, like working people.

Oh Euro, My Euro

Oh euro, my euro, 'twas said your time had come,
You'd withstood all the early flack, your doubters seemed undone;
With francs a ghost, with liras toast, and deutschmarks just a mem'ry,
Around the globe, your worth was sold, in circles monetary.
But now, alas, that time has past,
A new day has arrived,
With traders asking could it be
The euro won't survive?

Oh euro, once mighty, the money pack outpaced,
You made Dutch guilders disappear, pesetas you replaced;
With you baguettes were freely bought, with you paella ordered,
'Twas heralded no exchange rates, a Europe without borders.
Good euro, hope bringer
Have you become unsound?
You're even trading lower now
Than the beat up British pound!

The euro keeps on falling, it cannot find its legs,
Its strength has got so faded that it breaks through all the pegs;
The thinking here is changing fast,
As the richer lands gets rolled,
Could this have been a pretty dream,
One greatly oversold?

Exotics (a.k.a. Exotic Derivatives):
Derivative deals so crazy that only quants (See Quant below) could have created them and justified their inherent worth. Examples include hamster warrants, underwater convertibles with reset features, et. al.

Executive Performance Pay:
A kind of conceptional art project, perhaps the only such project that actually financially benefits the artist performers.

F

Faith-Based Economics:
Assuming that someone is actually guarding a store that keeps getting robbed, and the shelves of this store are still filled with unspoiled goods.

Fannie Mae & Freddie Mac: (SEE: **Maes** below)

Federal Reserve (a.k.a. The Fed):
An institution with no discernible means of support that has nevertheless acquired more than three trillion dollars in assets; an institution whose primary mission is to make charitable contributions to companies on Wall Street.

Financial News:
All the market news that's fit to print — provided it dovetails with the interests of the owners of the media doing the printing.

Financial Planners: (SEE: Retirement Planning)

Financial Planning:
Wishes structured as numbers.

Financial Poetry:
A quirky medium to describe doings in financial markets, and a
specialty of this book's author.

Fiscal Cliff:
An economic precipice with potentially awful consequences
where a country can find itself when its national legislature (or
even one chamber of that legislature) is dominated by ideological
dingbats.

Float:
Money you make because the guy who should have made it didn't
act fast enough.

Flipper:
A 1960s TV show about a happy dolphin who saved lives; in
more recent decades, a speculator in the real estate market who
buys houses to resell as quickly as possible to other flippers, with
the last flipper holding the now vastly over-valued property taking
a bath when the bubble pops.

Food Banks:
Repositories of the ultimate hard asset (food) whose reserves,
unfortunately, are not regularly inflated by a Federal Reserve that
only provides restocking services to investment banks.

Fracking:
A chemical enema inserted into the earth in hopes of releasing
large quantities of combustible flatulence.

Free Trade:
Very costly exchanges between nations in terms of environmental
and worker protections.

Full Disclosure:
Disclosing the least possible information consistent with avoiding
a felony conviction.

G

Glass-Steagall:
The perfect answer to the question of how to safeguard this country's financial system that no one in Washington any longer has the guts to mention.

Globalization:
A process that brings all peoples everywhere together in a common tragedy of epic proportions.

Going Public:
A process akin to flashers exposing parts of themselves they desperately hope will impress; in the stock market, carefully tailored perspectuses instead of trench coats provide the glimpses.

Gold:
A metal that markets often disdain because it doesn't compare well in market value to stocks, bonds, derivatives, and other paper assets, but a metal that many individuals nonetheless find endlessly appealing because they think paper-based market values are rigged and untrustworthy.

Golden Slacks:
A naughty reference to Goldman Sachs, which itself is not infrequently naughty (SEE: the adventures of Selig Cartwright, Goldman Sachs washroom attendant, below).

Golden Parachutes:
Devices that assure soft personal landings for corporate pilots whose ineptitude caused their companies to crash.

Grover Norquist.:
The Republicans anti-taxman.
Gross Domestic Product: (a.k.a. GDP)

The sum total of wealth accumulated by the richest two percent, modestly increased by crumbs allocated to everyone else.

The Grover Norquist Poem

Grover, Grover, G.O.P. drover
How does your congress vote?
To never switch, on tax the rich
Instead the poor to smote.

H

Hamptons:
A seasonal gathering spot of Wall Street's most successful and shameless, where past predations are boasted about and future ones planned.

Hard Assets:
Things of value you can see and touch, as contrasted with assets that are merely described and explained.

Health Care Costs:
A battleground of warring parties fighting to have others pay the costs of keeping people alive.

The Health Cost
Merry-Go-Round

Many states around the nation,
Face a budget situation,
Forcing them to do a fade,
When it comes to Medicaid.

ERs must pick up this slack,
Though resources they may lack;
Hospitals can't dodge the cost,
Of new patients they've been tossed.

Their bottom lines to help restore,
Hospitals must others gore;
Where to look in health care's market?
Insurers are their chosen target.

Insurers to meet profit goals,
Raise their fees, which shrinks their rolls;
Drop outs who can't pay this fee,
When they're sick to ERs flee.

This pass along, this circle wend,
Can really have but one true end;
Forget fond hopes 'bout where it's headed,
To rationing this game is wedded.

Hedge Funds:
Financial institutions built around the notion that the bigger
the fees paid to fund managers, the bigger the returns will be to
investors.

High Frequency Trading (SEE: Churning)

I

Inflation:
An excess of money in circulation so extreme that even poor
people have more of it than usual.

Inflation Rate:
The basis of mandatory increases in certain government
programs (like Social Security), hence a natural statistical target
to be finagled downward by those who wish to cut government
spending without appearing to do so.

Initial Public Offerings (a.k.a. IPOs):
Privately owned companies heavily rouged and tarted up
by skilled investment banker makeup artists for a one-time
appearance at a Wall Street coming out party.

Institutional Investors:
Professional groups entrusted with other people's life savings in
hopes they won't disappoint — hopes that occasionally actually
pan out.

Interday Highs:
Stimulant generated euphoria experienced by Wall Street traders
after brief washroom visits.

Investment Advisor:
A man or woman who knows everything about various investments except their intrinsic worth today and how this worth will be perceived and valued in the future.

Investment Banks:
Private companies engaged in risky economic behavior that receive loans at near zero percent interest from The Fed and get bailed out by taxpayers if their investments go very awry; the you-should-be-so-lucky sector of the present day American economy.

J

Job Creators:
In real life, anyone who helps create jobs; in Republican mythology, very rich people.

Jobless Recovery:
An oxymoron rather like "sickly health," currently much favored by economists who still have their own jobs.

Jubilee:
A biblical forgiveness of debt every 49 years, freeing those whose slavery came about through indebtedness to their masters; a secular version of Jubilee, were it to happen today, would free bank debt slaves from their present state of peonage.

Junk Bonds:
Bonds

K

K Street: The real legislative capital of America, where the outlines of laws are filled in to accommodate the desires of the privileged. The following poem explains the basis of its power.

K Street Remembers
And Rewards

Some congressmen retiring
Are careful to be siring
Through legislative wiring
Fat paychecks they're desiring.

While elsewhere they are firing
On K Street they're still hiring
But for these jobs requiring
Past servicing untiring.

L

Leading Economic Indicators:
Ten plot lines that tell a story that only an economist could love.

Liabilities:
Obligations you owe until you unload them in court (SEE: Bankruptcy) or via financial finagling (SEE: Derivatives).

Local Tax Lurkers

In town and city stores and streets
A tax collector lurks;
He's there to take his nibble
Where you parks or shops or works.

His hidden cam'ras tag you
If you try to beat a light,
And a ticket for jaywalking
He will issue day or night.

To litter now is criminal
And for this vile crime,
You may not end in jail
But you're sure to pay a fine.

To get your trash collected
Before it makes you gag,
There's a special service charge
'Cause he bills you by the bag.

God help the reefer smoker
That one's really gonna pay,
The lurker twicks and tweaks the law
And his house then takes away.

The lurker stiffs poor helpless folks
Who require his inspections,
And imposes fees and fines on stays
In the big house of corrections.

There's no way to avoid him
This ubiquitous bezerker
He'll nick and pick and stick you,
He's the local taxing lurker.

Finding The Right
Low Wage Haven

It used to be so easy to increase our money flow,
We'd move a plant from Tennessee to Northern Mexico,
And if that wasn't good enough we could always cut costs finer,
By finding a relocation site in far-off mainland China.

But then our chief competitor devised a slicker plan,
He moved soft goods production to a site in Pakistan,
When even that change didn't with his profit planning mesh,
He tapped the child labor pool in nearby Bangladesh.

The nice guy time was over, we got well and truly mad,
And got in touch with folks we knew who called the shots in Chad,
They guaranteed their workers would never ask for perks,
Their deal came with bosses who were former Belgium mercs.

We now believed our overhead was just too low to beat,
'Cause even the world's poorest have sometimes got to eat,
We thought below Chad's wages you would have to be a slaver,
Alas we had forgotten 'bout Andean prison labor.

We are but simple merchants, we merely seek to thrive,
And sell our wares in upscale shops that line Rodeo Drive,
But unfair competition may cause our firm to perish,
Or...
We could cut home staff wages—staff whose work we dearly cherish.

Liquidity:
Lots of money looking for good investments but willing to settle
for less if none are available.

Local Taxes:
Formerly based in real estate holdings, sales, and income, today
increasingly on gotcha fines and fees.

Low Wage Havens:
In world labor markets, as this poem shows, there's always some
people who will work cheaper.

M

Madoffism:
Living proof that while you can't fool all of the people forever,
when all of the people are federal regulators you can fool them for
a very long time.

Maes: A family of government-backed securities that like the
Brontes in another field is best-known for its female members—
Fannie, Ginnie and Sallie, all of whose lending excesses are
underwritten by American taxpayers. A male member of this
extended family, Freddie Mac, carries on a version of the family
business that services many of the same clients.

Marginal Tax Rates:
A measurement of one's obligations to government, "marginal"
in the sense that a good accountant can usually finagle you into a
smaller obligation category.

Market Friendly:
An unctuous display of good will toward Wall Streeters by pols
with their hands out for campaign contributions.

Michael Silverstein

Market Music:
Converting market movements into a musical idiom and then "composing" the market with this music for predictive purposes. An invention of Michael Silverstein, this book's author, who has never actually made a nickel with this invention but retains high hopes of doing so one day.

Market Regulators:
Financial Keystone cops who avoid political traffic accidents by never actually chasing the robbers.

Market Research:
"Manny. This is Hank over at Goldman. How's it going? What do hear about H.P.?"

Market Timing:
9:30 a.m. to 4 p.m. on weekdays.

Maturity:
A characteristic of people wise enough to know that when they hear the phrase from government officials and certified market mavens, "Maybe it really is different this time," it's time to cash out pronto.

Monetary Accommodation:
Nothing else is working, so let's try printing a lot more money and see what happens.

Monetary Policy:
Guessing how much money an economy needs and then guessing who should get it.

Monetizing:
Sometimes more really is less

Money Laundering:
A major profit center of major banks that find traditional ways to

earn (like making loans to small business) too onerous.

Moochers:
Anyone at the federal trough who isn't you.

Mortgage-Backed Securities:
A collection of debts that are often shaky individually, but nonetheless deemed secure when assembled and packaged in bulk.

N

Net Worth:
What you really have after deducting what you really didn't have.
New Normal:
The old poor.

O

Offshore Tax Shelters:
Where America's richest send their money to keep it from the clutches of evil tax collectors.

OPM (Other People's Money):
The key to success to almost any business venture, especially the Wall Street variety. Use your own money and you might lose some and become poorer. Use OPM and at worst you break even, but more often you make out well on fees from the venture no matter how it turns out, and with luck (and perhaps skill) make out still better with a percentage of the profits. Hedge funds are

the ultimate vehicles to tap this can't-lose mother load.

Opportunity Costs:
The costs of not doing what you could have done, maybe should
have done, but got talked out of doing.

Options:
A contact that allows its owner to buy or sell an asset at a certain
price — the strike price. These contracts have an expiration date,
however, and if you don't hit the strike price by then, you strike
out.

An Offshore Tax Shelters
Nod And Wink Poem

The Nod
My firm is big on patriotism
On ev'ry desk's a yellow ribbon
The boss can quote both Burke and Gibbon
We pay our taxes, that's a given.

The Wink
(Taxes are a real hooter
When you pay them in Bermuda.)

The Nod
We're sticklers when it comes to law
All crooks and cheaters we deplore
Our legal staffers make quite sure
With U.S. regs we're cool offshore.

The Wink
(There's a lot you gotta learnsy
When you set up shop in Guernsey)

The Nod
If Congress seeks to trim our pile
And says with Sam we've got to file
Our lobbyists employ their guile
To show this plan just ain't our style.

The Wink
(Ev'ry real corporate diva
Does his banking in Geneva.)

The Nod
There's no need for retribution
Prosecution's no solution
We achieve our absolution
With a campaign contribution.

The Wink
(Want a better bottom line?
Get your mail in Liechtenstein.)

P

Paris Hilton Tax: (SEE: Estate Tax)

Peonage:
Debt slavery; in present day America, college debt that can't be voided with personal bankruptcy. Here's a poem that sums up the whole ghastly peonage thing on these fair shores.

Petroleum:
The basic fuel of industrial societies, and the basic power that runs American politics.

American Peon

The banks sold you on plastic,
Said your life it would enrich,
Hyped the glories of free spending,
Never hinted at a hitch.
They were quick to raise your limits,
Made it all seem so sublime,
You could live above your income,
Pay in driblets over time.

Of course there were some drawbacks,
Fees and fines for paying late,
That caused a growing balance,
Ever faster to inflate.
Over time the easy payments,
Morphed into a challenge hard,
Though each mail brought an answer,
Offers for another card.

But alas, life ain't no picnic,
It can throw a nasty curve,
Your job gets shipped to China,
Illness strips your cash reserve.
And suddenly the plastic,
That let you dine out at the Ritz,
Gets used to pay the phone bill,
And for purchasing some grits.

All at once the banks are on you,
First they trash your credit score,
Soon they come for all they loaned you,
Come for that, and more, much more.
They have gamed the legal system,
They have paid their Congress dues,

They control all of the levers,
It's a lock...they win...you lose.

Now the masters of the plastic,
Have you well and truly pinned,
And they cunningly convince you,
It ain't them, it's you that sinned.
So for them you now will labor,
Pay their quirky bloated toll,
Try to think what could have led you,
To this awful peon role.

Ponzi Scheme:
An investment whose only business is paying old investors with money provided by new investors; the illegal private version of most present day legal government finance.

Prospectus: (SEE: Going Public)

Private Equity Firms:
Companies that acquire other companies they aren't qualified to run, using money they shouldn't have been allowed to borrow.

Old Man Oil

Old man oil, that old man oil,
His careless doings, bring folks to boil,
But old man oil, such things don't roil,
He just keeps drilling along.

His power's mighty, his lobbies toil,
To see his planning, big spills don't spoil,
As they befoul, the seas and soil,
He just keeps drilling along.

You and me, we bitch and moan,
Watching the tube we whine and groan,
Though dead fish float, the air made stale,
This guy he never ends in jail.

Folks get ticked off,
From years of trying,
Of leaders shrugging,
While nature's dying,
And old man oil,
He just keeps drilling,
Along.

———————

Prosperity:
Temporary periods of national solvency between two economic downturns.

Public Service Unions:
What's causing all the financial difficulties faced these days by local governments? Here's the answer to that question according to some Republican state governors.

Those Evil Public
Service Unions

The unions are the problem,
They cost the public gobs,
Of money that would otherwise
Create free market jobs.
We need some strong correctives
To these socialist collectives,
'Cause the unions we reviles
Foster middle class lifestyles. (Horrors!)
These bad times can be good ones
To tramp down union blight,
In the name of fiscal sanity
Get the system moved hard right.

Q

Quant:
The last name of an English fashion designer and a Dutch flautist;
also a quantitative analysis practitioner.

Quantitative Analysis:
Applying the mathematical technique of stochastic calculus to
finance in such arcane and incomprehensible ways that even
other Wall Streeters who claim to be the best and brightest are
hoodwinked into letting you play with some of their clients'
money.

Quantitative Easing:
The last refuge of central bankers who has tried everything else and failed.

R
———

Real Estate Bubbles:
Unwanted economic occurrences signaled when the phrase, "it has to keep going up because they don't make it anymore" is commonly heard in investment circles.

Recessions:
Bad economic times, except for investment banks with good contacts at the Federal Reserve.

Recession Stock Rally:
A kind of financial road race in which all the drivers end up winning while most owners end up with big loses.

Regulatory Reform:
Changed investment requirements so watered down and riddled with loopholes that Wall Street's best and brightest (see definition above) aren't hindered in the pursuit of their unseemly and undeserved compensation packages.

Restructuring:
Turning the tainted chop meat of company assets into more market palatable corporate burgers.

Retirement Planning:
By guessing how long you will live, and guessing which assets will perform the best between now and when you die, and

guessing what emergencies might affect your assets between now and then in ways that might reduce or enhance your personal hoard, and guessing your marital status and the size of your family in coming decades and what this might mean to your asset accumulation, and guessing how government policies (monetization of national debt, changes in tax laws, et. al.) might affect your older age future, you can appropriately plan for that future. Unless, of course...

Right To Pollute: (SEE: Emissions Trading)

Right To Work (a.k.a. Right To Work Cheap):
Another one of those "rights" (like Right To Life, Gun Rights, et.al.) that maybe society would be better off if they were toned down, watered down, or maybe de-righted altogether.

Risk Profiles: What the East German Stasi used to have on all that country's citizens to monitor their political views; in today's America, what private data miners have in a quantity and quality that would have made a Stasi operative drool.

Rube Goldberg:
Cartoonist famous for producing exotic and overly convoluted contraptions supposedly designed to perform simple tasks — the apparent role model for Wall Street derivative creators and Beltway tax writers.

Rubin, Robert:
The smartest guy in a room filled with Wall Street's best and brightest (see Best and Brightest above). Also, the guy with the best haircut.

S

Santa Claus Rally:
A stock market rally promoted by Wall Street peddlers to investors who still believe that a fat guy in a red suit really does exist somewhere and bestows financial gifts on those who keep their faith in the peddlers' products.

Securitizing:
Locking in profits by offloading risks to others via cunning packaging.

Selig Cartwright:
A fictional Goldman Sachs washroom attendant used by the author of this book to illustrate some of the shenanigans of that investment bank and Wall Street generally. (See some of Selig's adventures below.)

Small Business:
In the real world, a marginal enterprise run by a poor schmuck who works eighteen hours a day but goes under in a few years anyway because its owner can't compete with Walmart on price or get a loan from a bank living off endless doles from the Fed but not passing along any of this largesse to those who really deserve it; in the world of Republican myth, however, a market dynamo run by two-fisted hero netting more than $200,000 a year who would hire like crazy if only government regulations were eased, or even better, eliminated altogether.

Shorting:
Betting on the downside after convincing the rubes to bet the upside.

Social Media:
Mechanisms to promote intimate relationships with people you don't actually know or actually meet, and generate marketing information to purveyors of things you don't actually need or can

actually afford to buy.

Social Security:
A government run insurance program for the old and disabled whose continued solvency and popularity infuriates certain political fringe groups.

Social Security Trust:
The world's largest single repository of federal government IOUs; an erstwhile nest egg for elderly Americans, long rifled by Beltway officials who have their own totally separate retirement system.

Socialism:
Formerly an economic system in which government owned the means of production, distribution and transportation; currently a term used to denigrate anything that in any way lessens the wealth of the super-rich.

Sovereign Debt:
The debt of governments that can always pay their bills when they still have the right to print their own currency, but can run into big problems when they become part of a joint currency zone (like the EU) where debt may have to be repaid with real money.

Stimulus Packages:
Financial cardiac care all too often administered to the already long dead.

Stock Speculators:
Gamblers occasionally comped by Wall Street gaming dens in the certain knowledge that the house always wins in the end.

Stress Test:
If it's still breathing, feed it.

Sub-Prime Loans:
Loans made to people who never expected to pay them back

by lenders who never expected to collect them but didn't care because they securitized away the collection risk to others.

Swaps:
One guy pays another guy to pay up on a loan made by the first guy if the borrower can't be bothered to do so. There are now several hundred trillion dollars involving such swaps, but there's no need to worry. This game is being played by the very best and brightest on Wall Street with government regulators looking on but not interfering. So what could possibly go wrong?

T

Taking A Haircut:
A term that describes what happens when an investor who expected a ponytail return from a deal has to settle for a high and tight.

Tax Code:
A sort of secular Talmud endlessly picked over by experts in a largely futile search for meaning, or more often, in search of inconsistencies that provide a means to ignore its creators' real intentions.

Tax Havens:
Tropical islands with no visible means of support, which nonetheless manage to boast main streets lined with banks and cadres of public officials driving Mercedes.

Tax Loopholes:
Small errors in the tax code, but nonetheless large enough to squeeze through a million dollar deduction.

Tax Reform:
A deliberate misnomer intended to disguise the fact that the tax code is being altered in ways that make the rich richer.

Tax State:
The terminal stage of a nation or an empire's economic life, during which all truly productive endeavors are subordinated to a government's need for revenues.

Tax Trashing:
If everyone hates paying taxes, why not do away with them altogether?

Technical Analysis:
Looking at past market movements to predict future market movements; an intellectual exercise whose primary value is providing well paying jobs for smart folks who might otherwise have to seek out very limited and generally low paid work as music teachers or theologians.

The City:
London's financial district and the ancestral home of England's Conservative Party.

The Street:
The term market pros use to characterize their own businesses, proclivities and interests, to distinguish these clearly from "Main Street" where lesser folk dwell and flourish to a far lesser extent.

Too Big To Fail (Often now simply rendered TBTF):
Financial obesity that unlike physical obesity does not shorten life but guarantees its perpetual continuation.

The Tax-Free
Nation Poem

Ollie Wendell Holmes once said 'bout taxes in this nation,
    They are the price we gotta pay to have civilization.
But recently I'm thinking that this rule we should relax,
'Cause I'd rather not be civilized than pay my income tax.

The money sinks of public ed,
The vet and welfare rolls,
The subsidies for geezer health,
Who needs these wasteful doles?

Our streets would have no pot holes
If we made them all toll roads,
Stock markets would go through the roof
Without dull legal codes.

To keep our armies solvent
We could send our soldiers plundering;
No revenue means Congress
Won't in spending realms be blundering.

Who needs a tax-based commonwealth?
For too long we've been scammed.
We'll each care for the things we like,
All other things be damned!

Trade Deficits:
Lots of goods for us, more business for them, everybody's happy.
For awhile, anyway.

Think Tanks:
Institutions, especially the conservative leaning ones, that play an enormous role in concocting the economic nostrums that animate policies in Washington. Who works at these outfits? Here's one think tanker's story.

Trickle Down Economics:
An economic theory that holds that at some point the very rich, so bloated with wealth, so satisfied with their acquisitions, so tired of increasing their holdings, they voluntarily dribble a bit down to lesser mortals.

Treasury Bill/Treasury Bonds (a.k.a. T-Bills/T-Bonds):
Government promises to pay back the money of investors with an interest add-on almost certain to be well below the official inflation rate and far less than the real rate of inflation.

Toxic Assets:
Assets that no sane individual wants but which government has a strange and endless desire to possess.

Trading Range:
A kind of shooting gallery for stock prices where the targets are always moving, often in ways that seem to make no sense.

Transparency:
A market term that expresses the wish of people who invested in deals they didn't understand to finally figure out where their investment went long after its value has mysteriously evaporated.

Transfer Tax:
A tiny tax on stock trades that if ever enacted would have a number of beneficial effects, including a heart burn epidemic among Wall Street's high frequency traders.

The Think Tanker's Tale

For many long years I felt ineffectual
A misunderstood and ignored intellectual
My theories (though brilliant) were hooted and hissed
By colleagues and others their value dismissed.
But still I did labor to make them more statable
In hopes that one day they'd become much debatable
And those that opposed them for reasons nefarious
Would meet a just fate that was most deliterious.

In the tank, in the tank, in my Beltway think tank
Part campus, part book barn, part nut house, part bank.

It's true a great thinker on great ideas thrives
But it's also quite true that we have private lives
To best change perceptions and settle old scores
We need the support of big buck sinecures.
The best thinking's done on a surfeit of calories
And tends to improve in tandem with salaries
This linkage ain't found in a staid university
Not to mention such places' diverting diversity.

In the tank, in the tank, in my Beltway think tank
Part campus, part book barn, part nut house, part bank.

It was only by chance that I found my true nesting
The place in my heart I had always been questing
I'd published a screed, arcane and voluminous
So riddled with bile, some tagged it bitumninous.
It seemed for a time to attract no attention
Except the occasional snide condescension
Until came that call from a hunter of heads
Who asked if I'd ever considered Op Eds.

In the tank, in the tank, in my Beltway think tank
Part campus, part book barn, part nut house, part bank.

I'd always deemed Op Eds a medium trivial
So compact one's points couldn't be unequivial
Yet write one I did, laced with fury and gumption
Too high-brow (I figured) for pop press consumption.
But turn up it did, on a blatt's viewpoints page
Where it went on to garner both pro and con rage
My head hunter pitched it to tanks with fat coffers
And got back a slew of paid thinker job offers.

In the tank, in the tank, in my Beltway think tank
Part campus, part book barn, part nut house, part bank.

I now have a slot as cushy as jello
I'm called a researcher and visiting fellow
I analyze trends, write books in a gush
All published before being pulped into slush
On TV they love me on talking head junction
A chicken and peas night is my fav'rite function
At fund-raising meets, rich egos I lather
With partisan factoids and scholarly blather.

In the tank, in the tank, in my Beltway think tank
Part campus, part book barn, part nut house, part bank.

I longed for a place where they pay by the syllable
Where spewing odd visions and ideas is billable
Where the kinkiest, crankiest, odd scheme devisors
Can train to become presidential advisors.
A shadowy power most people don't see
Is now wield by thinkers-for-hire like me
My nostrums are slick, and my come backs are rapid
Just perfect for pols whose own brains have gone vapid.

In the tank, in the tank, in my Beltway think tank
Part campus, part book barn
Part nut house, part bank.

———————

U

Uncle Sam:
Nickname of the U.S. government; Sam helps a lot of needy and deserving folks, but in recent years has also become a vacuum cleaner that picks up the trash spewed by Wall Street — and pays top dollar while doing so...

Underground Economy:
The only still functioning economy in several non-German members of the European Union.

Unemployment:
What you get a lot of when Wall Street is under-regulated, and trickle down economics fails to trickle.

Unions:
Institutions that create large numbers of jobs by creating middle class incomes for working people who spend it in local small businesses that do more hiring to accommodate this added spending.

V

Value Added Tax (VAT):
The last taxing gasp of a government that has run out of other ways to soak the public.

Vulture Funds:
Uninvited guests at a too long protracted economic banquet.

Uncle Sam The
Garbage Man

When bubbles pop and slickers flee,
When profits from their sport falls short,
"Too big to fail," becomes the plea,
And players to Big Sam resort.

Sam, Sam, the garbage man,
Jumped in when others madly ran.

The regs that would prevent bad routs
Are much disdained in heady times,
The market then its wisdom flaunts
Until a crash, and then it whines.

Sam, Sam, the garbage man,
Cleans up the mess because it can.

You wonder, though, how long this game
With public money can be played,
Will private greed such outlays tame
Or make it worse, just more delayed?

Sam, Sam, the garbage man,
A willing purse without a plan.

W

Wall Street:
A very wealthy, sparsely populated, gated community surrounded
by very angry hoards of people living in much diminished
economic circumstances.

Convictus

Trapped by a heartless SEC,
Condemned to the pit where the felons board,
I thank the lawyers who earned their fees
For my undiminished hoard.

Caught in the grip of nasty fate,
I might a lengthy sentence got,
But with the help of legal pros,
I did some time, but not a lot.

Beyond the cell, the bars, the wire,
Looms a record I'll always bear,
But with the p.r. choir I'll hire,
A brighter image will soon appear.

It's not important the stuff I did,
How crookedly I played the game,
I can buy out of a blighted past,
I am above a sense of shame.

Wall Street Bonuses:
Rewards for a job well done; also given to people who do a job badly if they are high enough up the corporate hierarchy.

Wall Street Felons:
These are guys (they're always guys) who usually see themselves as enterprising innovators, and when cornered by the law know that the penalty won't be harsh and they will still find social acceptance. They think the following, in other words...

Warren, Elizabeth:
Recently elected Senator from Massachusetts and appointed to the Senate Banking Committee — which could be a problem for Wall Street's self-described best and brightest because....

The Problem
With Liz Warren

The problem with Liz Warren
Are persistent scary rumors
That in dealing with big lenders
She might favor small consumers.

While the minnows of the Beltway
Prepping for the next election
Pretend always real caring
For consumers more protection;

Truth be told the likes of Warren
Get them hot under their collars,
Honest servants of consumers
Could cost minnows big bank dollars.

World Bank:
An institution run by countries that won't admit they can't run their own economies, for the benefit of other countries that can no longer deny that fact.

Worst Case Scenario:
The analysts' friend; something they don't envision happening but are putting on the record anyway so if it does happen they can say they predicted it.

Y

Yield:
This has two meanings — A cry of surrender, or, the income from an investment; the two have been combined these days for investors who put money into bonds that surrender hardly any income.

Yen:
Something you hope for, unless you're Japanese, in which case you already have some in your wallet.

Z

Zombie Debt:
Debt obligations, usually of the credit card variety, that are "dead" in the sense they can no longer be collected in court because of state statutes of limitation laws, but live on in the mail and via collection calls from bottom feeders who have bought this debt for a penny or two on the original dollar.

Selig Cartwright, Goldman Sachs Washroom Attendant

Ambrose Bierce had an exorbitantly contrived alter ego, Father Gassalasca Jape, S.J., who he used to spout off on a wide variety of subjects. This book features its own such character — Selig Cartwright, a contrived Goldman Sachs washroom attendant, to play the same role.

Here are a few of Selig's financial commentaries. They are structured as washroom conversations with an equally fictional Mr. B., a top Goldman executive. Following these exchanges you'll read how Selig deals with telephone bill collectors in his personal life.

Selig Explores The Mysterious World Of Quantitative Easing

(The scene opens in the executive washroom of Goldman Sachs. Washroom attendant Selig Cartwright has just finished his morning chores as Mr. B. comes by for his usual 10 a.m. refresher.)

You're looking chipper today, Mr. B. I thought all the layoffs on Wall Street would be getting you down.

Layoffs? Oh those. They're only in The Street's retail businesses with small investors or small businesses. Our derivative trade is booming.

Derivatives are that big a trading area?

Selig, Selig, Selig. There are more than $700 trillion worth of these financial products out there now. Trillions, man. This isn't chump change like the deals we did to help countries like Greece and Ireland in the past. Countries that now don't even appreciate all we did for them.

Funny about that, Mr. B. You think they'd be grateful.

A world of ingrates, Selig. Sometimes I wonder why we bothered.

Indeed, sir. But about derivatives. I thought that Dodd-Frank legislation was supposed to put a crimp in that trade. I mean, derivatives did almost bring down the world financial system a few years back.

Old news, Selig. Dodd-Frank could have been a problem for the derivatives market. But our lawyers are shaping the bill's actual regulations so we won't be all that bothered. The Fed's quantitative easing has also helped with the Dodd-Frank problem.

What is quantitative easing, Mr. B? It sounds mysterious.

Not at all, Selig. The Fed is buying $45 billion a month in Treasury securities and $40 billion a month of mortgage backed securities that are owned by Wall Street firms. By the end of 2013 it will own $4 trillion of these assets.

That's the first thing I don't understand. How can The Fed buy anything, Mr. B? It's not a business. It doesn't earn any money. How can it buy things?

The Fed doesn't need to earn money. It makes money. Kind of like printing it, except using more up-to-date tools. And this new money has value because it's ultimately backed by taxpayers.

Well that's certainly reassuring. But sir, doesn't creating new money out of whole cloth create inflation?

Ah, Selig. That's the genius of this present quantitative easy. This money doesn't get into places that cause inflation — at least not in places where the government measures inflation.

Why not?

Look at it this way, Selig. If this new money somehow ended up going to little people like you, little people earning your little incomes, the way central banks used to do it when they printed a lot more money, what would you do with that extra money?

Spend it, sir.

Exactly, Selig. Lots of little people spending lots more money on lots more things and you get inflation. But because more than half of it is being used to buy debt issued by the Treasury, and the other half is being used to buy Wall Street's mortgage debt, it doesn't get to greedy little people like you who could cause inflation — at least the way government measures inflation.

I guess we can all be grateful for that, sir. Kind of. By why is The Fed buying so much Treasury debt?

Because by buying so much of it, Selig, it can set the rates. Which The Fed sets very, very low. Near zero, in fact.

But don't most debt buyers want to get larger returns from higher rates?

Selig, dear felllow. That's one of the things that makes this Fed program so innovative. It's the reason everyone who follows what The Fed is doing is saying it's going where no central bank has ever dared to go before. By making new Treasury debt so cheap, The Fed helps insure that the government can keep running up huge deficits it can afford to service. If rates on new Treasury debt went up more, even a little more, all taxes collected would have to go toward debt servicing and they'd be nothing left for entitlements or the military.

You mean, Mr. B., one government agency is creating money out of nothing to buy another government agency's debt at near zero rates so this other agency can meet the bills of an otherwise essentially insolvent government of which they are both a part?

You see a problem here, Selig? A cause for worry?

Worry? Heck no. In fact now that you've explained that part of The Fed's quantitative easy strategy, I'm actually feeling a bit giddy. And I can hardly wait to hear why The Fed is buying all those Wall Street-owned mortgage backed securities.

It's doing that, Selig, so the banks' reserves situation improves, and they can start lending more to small businesses. Which would do a lot to boost the economy — if it happened.

If it happened? You mean it hasn't happened?

Well, no, Selig. Banks don't want to lend to small businesses anymore because that's too risky and they might lose money. They couldn't do it even they wanted to because government bank regulators have mandated they can't lend too much to risky enterprises since that would endanger their reserves positions, and the economy is still so weak that smaller enterprises tend to be risky ones.

So if banks are trading their junky mortgage backed securities for triple-A government ones from The Fed, Mr. B, and this improves their reserves position, and these improved reserves aren't being used as collateral to boost small business lending, what are banks doing with this added investable capital?

Investing it in buying stocks, of course, keeping that market flying high. Sinking it in commodity trading, keeping that market fired up. And maybe most of all, using it to take the edge off Dodd-Frank and that law's efforts to slow down the growth of the derivative market.

I don't understand, sir.

The Dodd-Frank law, Selig, mandates that parties that take on the passed-along debt from other parties must have the capital reserves they'd need to pay up if this debt goes bad. The extra quality of reserves generated by The Fed's mortgage backed bonds buying program allows Wall Street firms to have the needed reserves for more derivative deals.

I think I finally understand quantitative easing, Mr. B. May I run it by you one more time to see if I have it all down right?

Of course, Selig. I live to serve. Provided it doesn't keep me from my private Stall # 8 for too much longer.

O.K, sir. Here goes. A government agency, The Fed, which is really just a few unelected people, can create $4 trillion of new money without approval from anyone else in government or anywhere else.

Right.

And it can use it to buy the debt of another government agency at the lowest possible interest rates.

Right.

And if this other government agency didn't have these unbelievably low rates, the federal government would soon not be able to afford to do anything but pay principal and interest on its new and old existing debt.

Right.

And the other part of quantitative easing, the buying mortgage backed bonds from Wall Street firms, that is supposed to be a stimulus package that helps small businesses, is pretty much a total failure for this purpose.

Right.

But what this mortgage debt buying does instead is allow Wall Street firms to keep stock and commodity markets trading flying high, and derivative packaging and peddling of the sort that almost destroyed the world financial system in the past to expand even further.

Right.

And if this expansion leads to an even bigger bust in world markets, The Fed would still be on the hook to do a bail out of the big banks.

How could it not, Selig?

And none of this $4 trillion easing causes inflation of the kind the government measures because it doesn't measure puffed up stock and commodity markets, or profits generated from derivatives as parts of its inflation measuring.

Right, Selig. But I should mention that some of the extra profits that people on The Street make from this mortgage-backed bond buying goes into our own purchases of houses in swank sections of Manhattan and London where prices are going through the roof. People like me are experiencing that inflation, while little folks like yourself only see some when buying food because of our commodity gaming.

Lucky us. But quite a burden for you Wall Streeters, Mr. B.

A burden the best and brightest must endure for the common good, Selig. And don't you forget it.

Not likely, sir. Given the number of unemployed guys who have the washroom cleaning skills one needs to do my own job.

Very prudent attitude, Selig. I no longer wish to endure not using Stall #8, however. Is it ready to receive.

Cleaned, stocked and ready, sir.

Good man. I'm going in.

Selig Cogitates About
Global Warming

Mr. B. You're late this morning. Forget to take your bran flakes with breakfast?

Just too busy to get away sooner, Selig. Following the energy bill before Congress. It's back on the front burner because of what happened in the Gulf of Mexico. And thankfully its global warming provisions have not been dropped. That could have cost us money.

I don't understand, sir. I don't understand why global warming is of special interest to Goldman Sachs.

That's because you don't understand the company's inner workings, Selig.

Beg to differ, sir. No one understands the company's inner workings better than the washroom crew.

Point taken, Selig. What I mean is that Goldman stands to make big money, really big money, if an energy bill containing certain provisions that are supposed to reduce global warming becomes law — if the bill lets polluters buy and sell credits allowing them to keep from cleaning up their polluting act. Someone would then have to handle the emission credit trading business, and investment banks like ours are all lining up to do the dirty — so to speak. We're talking mega bonuses for our traders here.

Not to be disparaging, Mr. B. but that's crazy. I mean, if you want to stop companies from polluting, you just enforce laws better. You fine them more to make them stop. You don't let them buy the right to pollute.

Selig, Selig, Selig. Not to throw disparaging back at you, but you still haven't fully entered the world of counter-intuitive Wall Street thinking. Commonsense would have kept us from promoting lending to people and governments that couldn't possibly pay it back. But did that stop us? Heck no, and we made a ton of money in consequence. Now, instead of being locked into the old 'cap and enforce' way of thinking to reduce polluting, we're pushing 'cap and trade,' the counter-intuitive solution to pollution, a trading approach that brings the mighty power of the market into play to save the planet. And a whole lot of new cash to The Street.

And the Administration and Congress went along on this for a while?

Went along? For a while they loved it! They were going to tax the pollution credits we peddled. Make it a cap, trade, tax plan. Everyone would win. Except now people in Washington have gotten a little queasy about our great cap and trade idea. They relabeled it 'carbon pricing,' but the public still isn't buying. Now an energy bill might not even include cap and trade.

I know that hurts Wall Street, sir. But would that really be bad for the environment?

Good question, Selig. I'll have to give that one a lot of thought. For now, did that new batch of green magazines I requested arrive?

On the shelf in your private Stall #8, sir. Next to the new Esquire and GQ.

I'll check 'em out right now, Selig. We're all thinking green these days, you know.

Selig Seeks To Tap
The Capital Markets

What's going on here, Selig? This washroom is a mess. There are things spread out all over the floor. It looks like you're holding a yard sale.

Not a yard sale, Mr. B. I'm doing a product roll out,

A product roll out? Whose products? What products?

My products, sir. The Selig Cartwright line of gotta-have-em washroom accessories. Items that turn your lavatories into showplaces. Like these seven different toilet plungers. The perfect tool for every plunge-worthy occasion.

What sort of occasions are you contemplating with these things, Selig?

Well, sir, suppose you...

Stop right there, Selig. I'm catching your drift. But what about that thing that looks like an M-16 water shooter that kids play with?

That's my Ferocious Bathroom Freshener, sir. It fires hi-test deodorizer. The stream can't penetrate a bathroom stall's steel door, but if your odor target is twenty yards away and you don't want to approach it at closer range, this is your baby. And look at all the differently shaped bowl brushes I have displayed. Would you like to try one out, Mr. B?

No Selig, That's not what I want. What I want is to know why you're displaying these extraordinary products here in the washroom of an investment bank?

Because of what you've been telling me all these years, Mr. B. That investment banks exist to bring new companies with innovative products to market. That you're in the business of raising capital for companies that make products like those you see here.

I'm touched you listened to me so closely, Selig. Really touched. I should have mentioned, though, that more than 70 percent of investment banks' money these days isn't made from bringing new companies to market, but from high frequency trading with money we get dirt cheap from the Fed. And that the capital we do raise isn't for small businesses like your own, which make up the bulk of the economy, but for giant businesses that bring in huge fees to us.

Like that wonderful Facebook deal, sir?

Like that one, Selig. But I am nonetheless touched by how my chatter over the years has inspired you, especially when I spoke about an opportunity economy.

Thank you for that, sir.

So I'm going to give you an opportunity now, Selig. An opportunity to clear all this junk out of this washroom in the next 15 minutes. And if you succeed in doing this before I return at that time, you will have the opportunity to retain your present position.

A sort of trickle down opportunity. sir.

Welcome to the New America, Mr. Cartwright.

Mr. B Sees The
Writing On The Wall

Good, lord, Mr. B. You're white as a sheet. What's the matter, sir?

They did it again, Selig. They spray painted those nine horrible words on our front entrance. You must have seen them when you came to work this morning.

No, sir. Don't you remember? Only top earners can use the front entrance these days. You made that a rule a few years back to give the rest of us something to aspire to.

Right. I remember now. So I guess you didn't see those spray painted words when you came to work. Our security people wash them off every day. But they keep reappearing again and again like some kind of awful warning.

What are they, sir? These nine words that fill you with such obvious foreboding?

"You have been judged, and Glass-Steagall is wanted."

Interesting mix of Bible and economics, sir.

Interesting, Selig? Horrifying! Glass-Steagall was one of those socialist laws passed during the New Deal to prevent the kind of market meltdown that triggered the Great Depression. It took us until 1999 to get that damn law off the books. It was cramping innovation. Putting a lid on our risk taking profits. The Volcker Rule they're trying to push down our throats these days is bad enough. But Glass-Steagall...

I don't know about that, Mr. B.

Don't know about what, Selig? You do believe in innovation,
don't you?

Of course, sir.

And in risk taking to bring new companies and new industries on
line?

Absolutely, sir, Except...

Except what, Selig?

I just don't understand why you don't want Glass-Steagall to
come back, sir. I mean, what I've heard is that it just separates
retail and commercial banking that are insured by the government
to protect bank depositors, just separates them from risk taking
ventures whose aim is to make the biggest possible profits.

That's right, Selig.

So what's the problem, Mr. B? If the government brings back
Glass-Steagall, it wouldn't have to regulate Wall Street so heavily
because the government, the taxpayers, wouldn't have to bail out
Wall Street companies if you lose a lot of money — you wouldn't
be under the same corporate umbrella as regulated institutions
whose depositors aren't risk takers and have to be saved at all
costs. It looks to me like a good deal for everyone. Separation
would free the government from an obligation to bail out risk
takers. Risk takers wouldn't have to be regulated as much because
they would no longer be a risk to anyone but themselves.

Selig, Selig, Selig. That's so, so...

Commonsensical, sir? I'm sorry.

No need to apologize, Selig. Common sense is a failing one sees
a lot on Main Street. Only a relatively few of us on Wall Street, in
Washington, and at some think tanks are blessed with the ability
to think counter-intuitively. To transcend common sense. To see

beyond the obvious.

What do you see beyond the obvious, Mr. B?

What I see, Selig, is opportunities. I see a future where every American has a shot at being able to feast regularly on caviar and truffles.

Sort of like a chicken in every pot, sir?

Yes, Selig. And a BMW in every garage, too.

A garage that hasn't been lost to bank foreclosure, sir, along with the adjoining house?

Right again, Selig, You've summed up my vision perfectly. Now let's get back to more immediate matters. Do you have any suggestions about how to keep those nasty nine words from greeting me and other top earners when we come to work?

You could erect a scaffold by the front entrance, sir. To scare warn off taggers.

Good, Selig, but too extreme. At least for the time being. Other ideas?

Well, sir, if the entire front of the building were made available to graffiti artists, another tag more or less would probably get lost in the mix. And passersby might even think that what's going on inside Goldman Sachs and other Wall Street investment banks was actually a government subsidized conceptual art project.

Selig, your chances of ever coming to work through that front entrance have just taken a steep nosedive. Is my Stall #8 ready for use?

Ready and waiting, sir. And the only writings on its walls are Post-It notes from my wife thanking you for keeping me out of the house all day.

Selig Faces A
Washroom Budget Crisis

Mr. B. Thank heavens you came by.

Of course I came by, Selig. I always come by at about this time. Is my usual Stall #8 ready?

Afraid not, sir. I got distracted. Got busy on something else — on trying to understand what to do about the memo that got slipped under the washroom door this morning.

You mean the cost cutting memo. It's the same memo that all our department heads are getting.

I'm a department head, sir? I didn't know that.

Yours is one of our less publicized departments, Selig. Not one we feature in our quarterly reports, but a department nonetheless. And since you're the only one I've ever seen down here who wasn't just visiting, I suppose you're its head. So what's your problem with that memo? It's pretty straight forward. Every department has to cut its spending 15 percent because of setbacks in the market.

But where am I supposed to make spending cuts, Mr. B? This is a washroom. People come here to...

Yes, yes, Selig. I know why we come here. You need a cost cutting suggestion to meet your new budgetary requirements? Alright. Here's one. You could lay someone off.

But I'm the only one who works here, sir.

In which case such a layoff would show real dedication to corporate interests, and would be recognized as such by top management. Of course, provisions would still have to be made by you to see the place remains clean and well stocked. If you can't lay off anyone, just reduce salaries and benefits.

I guess I could do that, sir. But couldn't I simply stop the subscriptions to GQ and Esquire for your personal Stall #8 instead, and stop ordering the DVDs for your visits there.

Interesting notion, Selig. Innovative, too. I'm glad to see you're looking at all possibilities when it comes to needed spending cuts.

You mean I can reach my goal that way, sir? I can stop getting the special items for your personal washroom stall in order to reach a 15 percent spending reduction?

Afraid not, Selig. Let me explain. We all have to suffer in difficult times, big people and little people alike. But not all suffering is equal. Folks like yourself suffer in financial terms, which I've heard can be difficult. Our own suffering is of a different order, a higher order. We have to endure things like hearing the President of the United States sometimes say unpleasant things about us. Hurtful things.. Things that make us feel...feel...

Good heavens, Mr. B, you're crying. I had no idea the best and brightest of Wall Street were so sensitive.

Sniffle. Sniffle. We don't show it often, Selig. It's just that sometimes, especially during the campaign season, some politicians are so darn cruel. Well, never you mind. I'll just soldier on. A Wall Streeter's gotta do, what he's gotta do. And now that I've let you see a part of me few others have ever seen, Selig, get my Stall #8 ready. And get your department's budget down 15 percent without saying things that make my personal suffering even worse.

Can Selig Save
Goldman's Image?

Mr. B. Back again this afternoon? Been eating tacos again for lunch?

No, Selig. I've come to see you.

Me, sir?

Yes you, Selig. Ever done any media?

Well, I was included in a New Kybo Monthly story a few years back about advances in sanitary hand drying. And...

No, Selig. Media. Real media. Television. Ever been featured in a TV ad?

Not that I remember.

Well, how would you feel about doing one for Goldman Sachs?

You want me to do an ad showing off those hand drying techniques I talked about in New Kybo Monthly? Or maybe one telling people how you let me invest my life savings in one of Goldman's synthetic CDOs?

No, Selig. And please keep your voice down when you talk about that exciting investment opportunity. Look, here it is in a nutshell. We took a beating in those Senate hearings the other day. People we've been supporting with hard cash for years turned on us like, like...

Frightened weasels, sir?

Exactly. So now we need an image refurbishment. Something that lets people know that Goldman Sachs isn't just a bunch of bonus crazed traders who can borrow cheap because we finagled ourselves into a commercial bank arrangement that also guarantees we get bailed out every time we overdo our financial innovations.

That's not the Goldman Sachs I know down here in the company washroom, sir.

Of course it's not, Selig. We're people people who know there's more to life than just making more money than everyone else on Wall Street. And we need a Main Street-friendly image to show that in a new TV ad campaign. We need a person out front who doesn't immediately bring to mind someone in a thousand-dollar suit who thinks he has a God-given right to huge compensation even when most everyone else in the country is hurting badly because of a few perfectly forgivable and understandable but much maligned investment gambits.

An ordinary sort of person, sir? A different image for Goldman? Something that tells the world that Goldman is as much at home in a washroom as a stock and bond-trading floor?

Exactly! So, Selig, what would you say to wearing a gleaming white tee shirt, sporting an earring, having a gold tooth inserted in your mouth to pick up studio lighting, and having your head shaved? Would you be willing to do that for Team Goldman?

Of course I would, Mr. B. I'd be honored to be Goldman's Mr. Clean. I may be a little scrawny for the tee shirt, though.

Our 33rd floor gym can take care of that. Even been there? Done the tanning parlor? Had a chance to chat with John Boehner keeping his own color up?

We have a gym? A tanning parlor? Whose John Boehner?

Never mind. A couple of days up there, you'll look like Charles Atlas fresh from a few weeks in The Islands. The TV guys can also hide your scalp eczema.

You'll supply the tee shirt, too, sir?

They'll be a three-pack delivered tomorrow morning. And any you don't use for the shoots you can keep for yourself. Because when someone deals with Goldman Sachs, Selig...

I know, sir. I know. We're family.

Selig Helps Set
Goldman's Standards

Mr. B. Surprised to see you in again today. And carrying all those papers.

They're for you, Selig.

Kind of you, sir. But I'm already well stocked with paper down here. Single ply. Double ply. Quilted. We got a new shipment of Charmin in the other day if you'd like to...

No, Selig. These are papers for you to read. To read. Didn't you get the memo?

Another memo? In the washroom?

Whatever. The thing is, Selig, the Goldman board is creating a business standards committee to examine our businesses practices, and we're looking to broaden its membership.

I don't understand, Mr. B. Why would anyone think Goldman Sachs should change its business practices? The idea is absurd.

Of course it is, Selig. But with all the misunderstanding about the way we've been operating that you read in the press these days...

You mean like slicking that A.I.G. deal, sir? Becoming a commercial bank to access cheap loans from The Fed? Helping Greece fool its way into the EU and threatening Europe's entire economy in consequence? Those bonuses you've been giving yourself? Those misunderstandings?

Yes, Selig, those misunderstandings. Personally, I can't fathom why any fair-minded person would quibble about such things.

These are certainly confusing times we live in, sir.

True enough. In any case, Selig. We want to tap a few outsiders, ordinary little people like you, to help with reshaping our company operations. Are you game?

I don't know, Mr. B. My work here in the washroom, it just involves maintaining the high-tech stalls, distributing super sanitized hand towels, keeping the luxury fixtures well shined. It's really just putting a fancy gloss on functions people don't want made public.

You're just the man we're looking for, Selig. By the way. When you come to the board meeting on the 40th floor, wear what you're wearing now. We're all just Main Street folks up there.

And you'll keep me on the memo list, sir?

Consider it done. Because whether you're a client or an employee, Selig, when you deal with Goldman Sachs...

I know, sir. I know. We're all part of the family.

Selig Hears The
Music Of The Markets

Mr. B. You're looking radiant. Today's visit to Stall #8 seems to have touched you in a very positive way.

It has, Selig, It has. What was that wonderful music I was listening to with my headphones in there? It was so...so...

Strangely recognizable, sir? Uplifting? A perfect accompaniment to your reading of this month's cover story in Bloomberg Markets Magazine?

Yes, Selig, And so much more appropriate than my usual listening choice in there.

Better even than Wagner's "Ride of the Valkyries," sir? Your usual listening favorite? That's high praise indeed, Mr. B.

Don't get me wrong. Selig. Wagner is certainly bowl-worthy. But this new music...What was it?

"Dow 2007," sir."

"Beg pardon."

I have a friend, sir. who composes the stock market. He takes charted stock movements, converts them to musical notation, adds a few jazz riffs, and creates a kind of music.

That's amazing, Selig. I don't suppose this technique also has predictive qualities. I mean, technical analysts in the market look at charts of stock movements searching for certain patterns they

say predict which way the market — and certain stocks prices —
are headed. Has your friend ever tried something like this with his
market music?

He has, sir.

And have his predictions ever panned out?

Almost never, Mr. B. Though once in awhile...

Stop right there, Selig. I like that "once in awhile." If we were to
package this kind of advice with the right legal caveats, claim its
a kind of technical analysis that employs audial rather than visual
hints, I see possibilities.

You might even bet the other side of the trade, Mr. B., to ensure
Goldman wins either way.

Interesting notion, Selig. I'll run it by our Ethics Committee. In
passing, do you think we could afford to hire this friend of yours?

Afford to hire him, sir? He's a musician. He makes his rent
playing senior centers and bas mitzvahs. You can get him for a
year for what you paid for dessert at that trader's twenty-third
birthday party the other night.

Hmmm. Much to cogitate about here, Selig. Do you have another
market music tune from your friend that I can listen to?

I do, sir. Dow Fourth Quarter 2008. Though it has a funereal
sound, if you just want a bit of variety...

"That kind of variety I can do without, Selig. Hook me up one
more time with Dow 2007. And have your friend destroy this
other number. Believe me. No one wants to see, much less hear,
2008 played again.

Selig Learns The Truth:
Big Banks Now A
Branch Of Government

(When Mr. B. enters the Goldman Sachs washroom for his regular morning visit, he finds washroom attendant Selig Cartwright waiting expectantly...)

What is it, Selig? You look pensive. Is there something you want to tell me?

No, sir. Something I want to ask you. Do you vote, Mr. B?

Of course, I vote, Selig. It's every American's duty. We need to elect the best possible representatives who will make the best possible laws.

That's what I've always thought too, sir. Except now...now...

Now what, Selig? Speak up man.

It's some stories I've been reading in the New York Times, sir. Hearing elsewhere, too.

That rag. No wonder you're upset, Selig. What have they been writing now? I'll wager it's something nasty about big banks.

Yes, sir. They and other media are saying, well, hinting strongly anyway, that the people we think we're electing to make the best possible laws don't really make the laws that affect big banks. That the banks themselves, their lobbyists, their lawyers...

Stop right there, Selig. I know where this is going. They're saying that after the people in Washington we elect to make laws that are supposed to regulate Wall Street, then pass these laws along to other government officials to make the regulations that actually allow the laws to work, these other government officials end up negotiating with us, and we make sure these new laws don't work against our interests. Is that what your reading and hearing, Selig?

That's exactly what I'm reading and hearing, sir. Is it all lies?

Lies, Selig? Of course it's not lies. That's exactly the way things are done these days. What's the problem?

I guess the problem, Mr. B, at least for some people, is that companies and industries the government think have done things, or might do things, that require regulation to protect the public, shouldn't write these regulations themselves.

I could tell you a lot of reasons that argument is silly, Selig. Instead, I'll just say what Dick Cheney said when it was pointed out that the overwhelming majority of Americans didn't think we should get into a war in Iraq.

What did he say, sir?

Cheney said just one word, Selig. He just said: "So."

I don't understand, sir.

What he was saying, Selig, was that no matter what most Americans thought or wanted, he and others in the Bush Administration had the power to start a war if they wanted to start a war. No one could stop them. They had the power and they could use it as they saw fit. And if most Americans disagreed, thought it was stupid, thought it would lead to disastrous consequences, So.

You mean, Mr. B., that Washington passed Dodd-Frank to keep Wall Street from operating the way it wants to operate, and people are disappointed because you're putting the kibosh on its effective enforcement.

So.

And Americans are furious because the big banks made a record $40 billion-plus in the first quarter of this year while average wages and benefits for other Americans, even the ones who still have a job, are stagnant or falling.

So.

And if Democrats instead of Republicans are in power, when it comes to really keeping Wall Street in check, both end up going along with what Wall Street wants.

So.

Which makes present-day politics, at least when it comes to Wall Street, irrelevant. No matter who seems to be in power, you're in power when it comes to things that involve your own interests.

So.

And that in essence, sir, Wall Street has become a fourth branch of government with powers equal to the other three branches on critical economic matters.

An equal branch of government, Selig? Are you trying to be offensive?

No, sir. I just meant...

Selig, Selig, Selig. They're on the phone every day begging us for money they think they need to get reelected. They're sucking up to us daily so they can get fat pay goodies after leaving office. We're funneling money to their family members directly or indirectly if they play along with what we want. All the people who argue our case on legislation, and negotiate regulations, are their ex-employees — or former colleagues. Yes, Selig, we're a fourth branch of government. But equal? Let's just say some branches are more equal than others.

Now I understand present-day American politics, Mr. B. I'm still a little confused about something, though. You told me just a few minutes ago how important it is to vote? But if you control so much and you're not voted into an office, why is voting still so important?

Because, Selig, when the next big crash comes, the blame is going to fall on people who were supposed to make laws to prevent it. It's elected people who are going to take the blame. And when the next crop of pols replaces them, we'll still be free to buy them, too.

An inspiring explanation, Mr. B.

Yes, Selig. And one that should make you very proud. You're part of the big bank team, after all.

My cup runneth over, Mr. B.

See that it's the only thing in this washroom that so runneth. You'd be amazed how many job applications we get these days for jobs like yours, jobs cleaning Wall Streeter bathrooms.

I appreciate the opportunity to serve, sir.

Continue to do so, Selig. Now get my Stall #8 ready for use. Pronto.

Selig's Dealings
With
Debt Collectors

Selig Cartwright has a personal life that like so many other Americans has been made more perilous by debt. For years it was also made more irritating by calls during the dinner hour, not from telemarketers peddling wares of dubious worth, but from representatives of credit card-issuing banks dunning him for money owed on these cards.

Such calls are of course inherently silly. All debtors know they owe the money. Letters printed on garishly colored stock and other communications have informed them so with great frequency. If they could pay, they would pay. Why interrupt a weekday evening meal or a weekend nap to add to this useless cacophony?

Given the irritating and indeed irrational nature of these intrusions, Selig felt himself entitled to some fun at the expense of these would-be tormentors. True, they almost certainly had their own reasons to be unhappy, sitting in their wretched little cubicles wearing uncomfortable headsets and practicing a profession no sane person since the invention of the telephone had ever aspired to. But why take their failed existences out on me, Selig thought? Doing so was unkind and deserved appropriately unkind responses.

A few examples of these collector-unfriendly responses, in dialectic form, follow:

Getting Better Acquainted

Bill collector caller: You're going to hear from me a lot. I intend to keep calling until we get this settled.

Selig's response: That's awfully kind of you. I'm a shut-in and don't hear from many people these days. Tell me a little bit about yourself.

Payment Switch

Bill collector caller: Maybe it's time we had a long conversation and worked this thing out.

Selig's response: The longer the better. My calls are billed at $9.95 per minute. I'll need your credit card number and date of expiration to get us started.

Going Biblical

Bill collector caller: Don't you think you have a moral obligation to pay this debt?

Selig's response: I did until my pastor told me this is a Jubilee year and all debts are forgiven. Alleluia!

The Real Wimp

Bill collector caller: Why don't you stop complaining about hard times and just pay what you owe?

Selig's response: I didn't call you to complain. You called me to complain. You people make unsecured loans at outrageous interest rates and throw in a lot of nasty fees and fines. Now you can't collect. Suck it up. Stop whining. Take it like a man.

Reciprocation

Bill collector caller: I'm trying to help you.

Selig's response: Why would you do that? I don't want to help you.

Payday Lending

Bill collector caller: What will it take to get you to pay something on this card?

Selig's response: Well, since you're obviously working and I'm not, you could loan me a few hundred dollars until I get back on my feet.

About Courtesy

Bill collector caller: Don't you think you owe me the courtesy of discussing this debt?

Selig's response: No.

About The Author Of
The Devil's Dictionary
Of Wall Street

Michael Silverstein, National Public Radio's "Wall Street Poet," is a former senior editor with Bloomberg Financial News. Over the years his writing has run in many of this country's high profile media including The New York Times, Los Angeles Times, USA Today, The Wall Street Journal, et. al. These days it frequently appears on the Op Ed Page of The Philadelphia Inquirer.

Other e-books by Silverstein currently available on Amazon include: *Fifteen Feet Beneath Manhattan*, a very funny comic novel about very strange doings under Gotham streets in the 1970s; *The Bellman's Revenge*, another comic novel, this one keying off every traveler's secret fear; and *Murder At Bernstein's*, the story of a financial news billionaire who wants to be elected Mayor of Philadelphia.

Follow Michael Silverstein at http://blog.wallstreetpoet.com/